foundations

SMALL GROUP STUDY GUIDE

taught by tom holladay and kay warren

SANCTIFICATION

ZONDERVAN®

SADDLEBACK CHURCH

ZONDERVAN.com/
AUTHORTRACKER
follow your favorite authors

Foundations: *Sanctification Study Guide*
Copyright © 2003, 2004, 2008 by Tom Holladay and Kay Warren

Requests for information should be addressed to:
Zondervan, *Grand Rapids, Michigan 49530*

ISBN 978-0-310-27684-5

Printed in the United States of America

08 09 10 11 12 13 14 15 16 17 18 • 23 22 21 20 19 18 17 16 15 14 13 12 11 10 9 8 7 6 5 4 3 2 1

foundations TABLE OF CONTENTS

FOREWORD

What *Foundations* Will Do for You

I once built a log cabin in the Sierra Mountains of northern California. After ten backbreaking weeks of clearing forest land, all I had to show for my effort was a leveled and squared concrete foundation. I was discouraged, but my father, who built over a hundred church buildings in his lifetime, said, "Cheer up, son! Once you've laid the foundation, the most important work is behind you." I've since learned that this is a principle for all of life: you can never build *anything* larger than the foundation can handle.

The foundation of any building determines both its size and strength, and the same is true of our lives. A life built on a false or faulty foundation will never reach the height that God intends for it to reach. If you skimp on your foundation, you limit your life.

That's why this material is so vitally important. *Foundations* is the biblical basis of a purpose-driven life. You must understand these life-changing truths to enjoy God's purposes for you. This curriculum has been taught, tested, and refined over ten years with thousands of people at Saddleback Church. I've often said that *Foundations* is the most important class in our church.

Why You Need a Biblical Foundation for Life

- *It's the source of personal growth and stability.* So many of the problems in our lives are caused by faulty thinking. That's why Jesus said the truth will set us free and why Colossians 2:7a (CEV) says, *"Plant your roots in Christ and let him be the foundation for your life."*

- *It's the underpinning of a healthy family.* Proverbs 24:3 (TEV) says, *"Homes are built on the foundation of wisdom and understanding."* In a world that is constantly changing, strong families are based on God's unchanging truth.

- **It's the starting point of leadership.** You can never lead people farther than you've gone yourself. Proverbs 16:12b (MSG) says, *"Sound leadership has a moral foundation."*

- **It's the basis for your eternal reward in heaven.** Paul said, *"Whatever we build on that foundation will be tested by fire on the day of judgment . . . We will be rewarded if our building is left standing"* (1 Corinthians 3:12, 14 CEV).

- *God's truth is the only foundation that will last.* The Bible tells us that *"the sound, wholesome teachings of the Lord Jesus Christ . . . are the foundation for a godly life"* (1 Timothy 6:3 NLT), and that *"God's truth stands firm like a foundation stone . . ."* (2 Timothy 2:19 NLT).

Jesus concluded his Sermon on the Mount with a story illustrating this important truth. Two houses were built on different foundations. The house built on sand was destroyed when rain, floods, and wind swept it away. But the house built on the foundation of solid rock remained firm. He concluded, *"Therefore everyone who hears these words of mine and puts them into practice is like a wise man who built his house on the rock"* (Matthew 7:24 NIV). *The Message* paraphrase of this verse shows how important this is: *"These words I speak to you are not incidental additions to your life . . . They are foundational words, words to build a life on."*

I cannot recommend this curriculum more highly to you. It has changed our church, our staff, and thousands of lives. For too long, too many have thought of theology as something that doesn't relate to our everyday lives, but *Foundations* explodes that mold. This study makes it clear that the foundation of what we do and say in each day of our lives is what we believe. I am thrilled that this in-depth, life-changing curriculum is now being made available for everyone to use.

— Rick Warren, author of *The Purpose Driven® Life*

PREFACE

Get ready for a radical statement, a pronouncement sure to make you wonder if we've lost our grip on reality: *There is nothing more exciting than doctrine!*

Track with us for a second on this. Doctrine is the study of what God has to say. What God has to say is always the truth. The truth gives me the right perspective on myself and on the world around me. The right perspective results in decisions of faith and experiences of joy. *That* is exciting!

The objective of *Foundations* is to present the basic truths of the Christian faith in a simple, systematic, and life-changing way—in other words, to teach doctrine. The question is, why? In a world in which people's lives are filled with crying needs, why teach doctrine? Because biblical doctrine has the answer to many of those crying needs! Please don't see this as a clash between needs-oriented and doctrine-oriented teaching. The truth is we need both. We all need to learn how to deal with worry in our lives. One of the keys to dealing with worry is an understanding of the biblical doctrine of the hope of heaven. Couples need to know what the Bible says about how to have a better marriage. They also need a deeper understanding of the doctrine of the Fatherhood of God, giving the assurance of God's love upon which all healthy relationships are built. Parents need to understand the Bible's practical insights for raising kids. They also need an understanding of the sovereignty of God, a certainty of the fact that God is in control, that will carry them through the inevitable ups and downs of being a parent. Doctrinal truth meets our deepest needs.

Welcome to a study that will have a lifelong impact on the way you look at everything around you and above you and within you. Helping you develop a "Christian worldview" is our goal as the writers of this study. A Christian worldview is the ability to see everything through the filter of God's truth. The time you dedicate to this study will lay a foundation for new perspectives that will have tremendous benefits for the rest of your life. This study will help you:

- Lessen the stress in everyday life

- See the real potential for growth the Lord has given you

- Increase your sense of security in an often troubling world

- Find new tools for helping others (your friends, your family, your children) find the right perspective on life

- Fall more deeply in love with the Lord

Throughout this study you'll see three types of sidebar sections designed to help you connect with the truths God tells us about himself, ourselves, and this world.

- *A Closer Look:* We'll take time to expand on a truth or look at it from a different perspective.

- *Key Personal Perspective:* The truth of doctrine always has a profound impact on our lives. In this section we'll focus on that personal impact.

- *Living on Purpose:* James 1:22 (NCV) says, *"Do what God's teaching says; when you only listen and do nothing, you are fooling yourselves."* In his book, *The Purpose Driven Life,* Rick Warren identifies God's five purposes for our lives. They are worship, fellowship, discipleship, ministry, and evangelism. We will focus on one of these five purposes in each lesson, and discuss how it relates to the subject of the study. This section is very important, so please be sure to leave time for it.

Here is a brief explanation of the other features of this study guide.

Looking Ahead/Catching Up: You will open each meeting with an opportunity for everyone to check in with each other about how you are doing with the weekly assignments. Accountability is a key to success in this study!

Key Verse: Each week you will find a key verse or Scripture passage for your group to read together. If someone in the group has a different translation, ask them to read it aloud so the group can get a bigger picture of the meaning of the passage.

Video Lesson: There is a video lesson segment for the group to watch together each week. Take notes in the lesson outlines as you watch the video, and be sure to refer back to these notes during your discussion time.

Discovery Questions: Each video segment is complemented by questions for group discussion. Please don't feel pressured to discuss every single question. The material in this study is meant to be your servant, not your master, so there is no reason to rush through the answers. Give everyone ample opportunity to share their thoughts. If you don't get through all of the discovery questions, that's okay.

Prayer Direction: At the end of each session you will find suggestions for your group prayer time. Praying together is one of the greatest privileges of small group life. Please don't take it for granted.

Get ready for God to do incredible things in your life as you begin the adventure of learning more deeply about the most exciting message in the world: the truth about God!

— Tom Holladay and Kay Warren

How to Use This Video Curriculum

Here is a brief explanation of the features on your small group DVD. These features include a *Group Lifter,* four *Video Teaching Sessions* by Tom Holladay and Kay Warren and a short video, *How to Become a Follower of Jesus Christ,* by Rick Warren. Here's how they work:

The Group Lifter is a brief video introduction by Tom Holladay giving you a sense of the objectives and purpose of this *Foundations* study on sanctification. Watch it together as a group at the beginning of your first session.

The Video Teaching Sessions provide you with the teaching for each week of the study. Watch these features with your group. After watching the video teaching session, continue in your study by working through the discussion questions and activities in the study guide.

Nothing is more important than the decision you make to accept Jesus Christ as your Lord and Savior. You will have the option to watch a short video presentation, *How to Become a Follower of Jesus Christ,* at the end of Session Two. In this brief video segment, Rick Warren explains the importance of having Christ as the Savior of your life and how you can become part of the family of God. If everyone in your group is already a follower of Christ, or if you feel there is a better time to play this segment, continue your session by turning to the Discovery Questions in your DVD study guide. You can also select this video presentation separately on the Main Menu of the DVD for viewing at any time.

Follow these simple steps for a successful small group session:

1. Hosts: Watch the video session and write down your answers to the discussion questions in the study guide before your group arrives.

2. Group: Open your group meeting by using the "Looking Ahead" or "Catching Up" section of your lesson.

3. Group: Watch the video teaching lesson and follow along in the outlines in the study guide.

4. Group: Complete the rest of the discussion materials for each session in the study guide.

It's just that simple. Have a great study together!

1

Session One

TWO FOCUSES OF SANCTIFICATION

LOOKING AHEAD

We all need to grow. None of us has "arrived" at spiritual perfection! As we start this study on personal growth, share with the group one or two areas where you would like to see growth in your spiritual life. Consider writing this expressed desire in the space below as a way of marking your request. Use it as a checkup later on to see what God is doing in your life.

Key Verse

With one sacrifice he made perfect forever those who are being made holy.

Hebrews 10:14 (NCV)

BIBLE TEACHING
Watch the video lesson now and take notes in your outline on pages 3–5.

As Believers We Have Been:

1. _____—Declared eternally not guilty. (Romans 5:1; Galatians 2:16)

2. _____—Being set apart for holiness. (1 Corinthians 6:11; 1 Thessalonians 5:23)

3. _____—The completed act of our being with God for eternity. (Romans 8:30)

Sanctified means _____ .

In the Old Testament it was most often the places and objects of worship that were called "set apart" for God's honor and use. In the New Testament it is God's people who are "set apart" for God's honor and use.

> *If a man cleanses himself from the latter, he will be an instrument for noble purposes, made holy, useful to the Master and prepared to do any good work.* (2 Timothy 2:21 NIV)

"Sanctified" comes from the same word as "saint." In the Bible, all believers are called saints.

I am not trying to grow toward sainthood. I am a _____ saint.

The doctrine of sanctification sets the foundation for our growth as Christians. One of the missing ingredients in our spiritual growth is an understanding of this doctrine. Without understanding the doctrine of sanctification, you can easily find yourself falling into the traps of trying to grow in Christ based on your own effort (legalism) or presuming on God's grace to grow you no matter how you live (license).

Two Focuses of Sanctification

The two focuses of sanctification refer to:

The _____ of being made holy

The _____ of becoming holy

1. Sanctification is _____ and _____ .

   And by that will, we have been made holy through the sacrifice of the body of Jesus Christ once for all. (Hebrews 10:10 NIV)

   Because of God you are in Christ Jesus, who has become for us wisdom from God. In Christ we are put right with God, and have been made holy, and have been set free from sin. (1 Corinthians 1:30 NCV)

2. Sanctification is _____ and _____ .

   Like newborn babies, crave pure spiritual milk, so that by it you may grow up in your salvation. (1 Peter 2:2 NIV)

   ... seek to live a clean and holy life, for one who is not holy will not see the Lord. (Hebrews 12:14 LB)

   Grow in the grace and knowledge of our Lord and Savior Jesus Christ. (2 Peter 3:18a NCV)

One verse sums up both:

> *With one sacrifice he made perfect forever those who are being made holy.* (Hebrews 10:14 NCV)

You express faith concerning these two focuses when you say: "I am a sanctified person who is being sanctified."

Sanctification is not the process of you trying really hard to become something that you are not. Sanctification is the process of beginning to live out what you already are.

DISCOVERY QUESTIONS

1. Based on ideas we may have acquired over the years, it might be difficult for us to think of ourselves as "holy," but Scripture says that's exactly what Christians are. With that in mind, what are some things we typically think make a person holy? Contrast these ideas with what God says make us holy.

2. Think about the term "set apart." Can you think of things that are set apart for a special use? How does that idea help you better understand holiness or sanctification?

3. What inner attitudes encourage and inspire your growth in Christ? What attitudes put up a barrier to your growth?

4. Discuss some ways that your group can support one another in the process of becoming like Jesus.

Did You Get It? How has this week's study helped you see both the finished action and the daily process of holiness?

Share with Someone: Think of a person you can encourage with the truth you learned in this session. Write their name in the space below and pray for God to provide that opportunity this week.

LIVING ON PURPOSE
Discipleship

Because this entire study is about spiritual maturity, the purpose activities over these next four weeks will focus on spiritual growth. Each week, we'll be asking you to participate in an exercise on one of four classic spiritual disciplines. The four topics we have chosen are: solitude, fasting, generosity, and confession.

This week's exercise is on **solitude.** It sounds simple, but you may find it more challenging than you'd think! Find a place where you can sit for twenty minutes and do nothing else but listen—NOT in your car as you're driving to work or your living room where you'll be interrupted by the phone or your kids! Choose a place where you can be entirely alone for twenty minutes and just listen. Ask God, "What do you want to say to me?" . . . and then just listen.

PRAYER DIRECTION

Take some time as a group to talk about your specific prayer requests and to pray for one another.

NOTES

2

Session two

THE TWO NATURES
OF THE CHRISTIAN

CATCHING UP

1. What did you learn during last week's "Living on Purpose" activity? Were you able to spend twenty minutes in solitude, listening to God? What did you experience as a result?

2. Did you notice that you were more aware of living holy and separate for Christ as a result of last week's lesson? Share any opportunities or insights you may have observed.

Key Verse

I have been crucified with Christ and I no longer live,
but Christ lives in me. The life I live in the body, I live by faith in
the Son of God, who loved me and gave himself for me.

Galatians 2:20 (NIV)

Two Natures of the Christian

You have both an _____ nature and a _____ nature.

A CLOSER LOOK
The Old and New Natures of the Christian

Your old nature, which the Bible also calls your "flesh," is your inner desire and tendency toward sin. It is not the feeling of being tempted; it is the inner part of who you are that inevitably will choose to say yes to various temptations. Before you became a believer, your old nature was your only nature. We all have this old nature—this natural propensity to sin—because of the fall of man that happened in the garden of Eden.

Your new nature was given to you the moment you gave your life to Christ. The new nature is the new life and new power to live that have been given to you because of your trust in what Jesus did for you through his death and resurrection.

One of the most crucial aspects of growth in our lives as believers is learning how to trust God concerning both our old nature and our new nature.

---

1. You express faith concerning your new nature when you see yourself

   as _____ .

   > *When someone becomes a Christian, he becomes a brand new person inside. He is not the same anymore. A new life has begun! [You are a new creation in Christ. The moment you believed in Christ as your Savior, a spiritual transaction happened that changed everything.]* (2 Corinthians 5:17 LB)

- I was "_____."

All of us were born in sin because we are Adam's descendants. We choose to sin because that is our spiritual nature. The Bible refers to our condition as being "in Adam," which means we were subject to judgment and death.

> *For as in Adam all die . . .* (1 Corinthians 15:22 NIV)

- I am now "_____."

Spiritual life is gained only through spiritual birth (John 3:6). The moment we were born again, our soul came into union with God because of Christ. We are now in Christ.

> *³Praise be to the God and Father of our Lord Jesus Christ, who has blessed us in the heavenly realms with every spiritual blessing in Christ. ⁴For he chose us in him before the creation of the world to be holy and blameless in his sight.*
> (Ephesians 1:3–4 NIV)

There are only two types of people in the world—those who are in Adam and those who are in Christ. You are in Christ if Christ is in you. An exchange of lives occurs: you give Jesus your life, and he gives you his.

Who Is This "New Person"?

I am a light in the world. (Matthew 5:14)

I am a child of God. (John 1:12)

I am Christ's friend. (John 15:15)

I am chosen and appointed by Christ to bear his fruit. (John 15:16)

I am a slave of righteousness. (Romans 6:18)

I am a joint heir with Christ. (Romans 8:17)

I am a temple, a dwelling place, of God. (1 Corinthians 3:16, 6:19)

I am a member of Christ's body. (1 Corinthians 12:27; Ephesians 5:30)

I am a new creation. (2 Corinthians 5:17)

I am reconciled to God and a minister of reconciliation.
(2 Corinthians 5:18–19)

I am a saint. (Ephesians 1:1; 1 Corinthians 2:1–2)

I am God's workmanship. (Ephesians 2:10)

I am a citizen of heaven. (Philippians 3:20; Ephesians 2:6)

I am righteous and holy. (Ephesians 4:24)

I am hidden with Christ in God. (Colossians 3:3)

I am chosen and dearly loved. (Colossians 3:12)

I am a son/daughter of light and not of darkness. (1 Thessalonians 5:5)

I am an enemy of the Devil. (1 Peter 5:8)

I am victorious. (1 John 5:4)

I am born again. (1 Peter 1:23)

I am alive with Christ. (Ephesians 2:5)

I am more than a conqueror. (Romans 8:37)

I am the righteousness of God. (2 Corinthians 5:21)

I am born of God and the Evil One cannot touch me. (1 John 5:18)

I am to be like Christ when he returns. (1 John 3:1–2)

KEY PERSONAL PERSPECTIVE
Truths to Help You Live Your New Life

1. You don't have to _____ your new life. This new life is a creation of God. It's not a matter of your trying.

   . . . you have clothed yourselves with a brand-new nature that is continually being renewed as you learn more and more about Christ, who created this new nature within you. (Colossians 3:10 NLT)

   We don't have to make ourselves new. We are to live out the new life the Spirit has already given us.

2. You don't have to work to _____ your new life. Your new life is kept with Christ in God.

   Your old sinful self has died, and your new life is kept with Christ in God. (Colossians 3:3 NCV)

   That is incredibly secure! We are kept with Christ and then it is put in God. That is security in security.

2. You express faith concerning your old nature when you see yourself as _____ .

   > *Your old sin-loving nature was buried with him by baptism when he died; and when God the Father, with glorious power, brought him back to life again, you were given his wonderful new life to enjoy.* (Romans 6:4 LB)

How do I "put off" the old nature?

- Not by _____

- Not by _____

- By faith in what _____

And since your old sin-loving nature "died" with Christ, we know that you will share his new life. (Romans 6:8 LB)

3. You express faith concerning both your new and old natures when you see yourself with a _____ to overcome evil.

- Before salvation, I belonged to _____.

   You belong to your father, the devil, and you want to carry out your father's desire. (John 8:44a NIV)

- After salvation, I belong to _____.

   And you also are among those who are called to belong to Jesus Christ. (Romans 1:6 NIV)

- Because I belong to God, Satan has no power to

   _____ .

   [8]Be self-controlled and alert. Your enemy the devil prowls around like a roaring lion looking for someone to devour. [9]Resist him, standing firm in the faith . . . (1 Peter 5:8–9 NIV)

God has not left our growth to chance. The foundation of your sanctification is nothing less than the death and resurrection of Jesus Christ. This means two things:

First, because of the power of Jesus' crucifixion, you no longer have to be controlled by your old nature.

   I have been crucified with Christ and I no longer live, but Christ lives in me. The life I live in the body, I live by faith in the Son of God, who loved me and gave himself for me. (Galatians 2:20 NIV)

Second, because of the power of Jesus' resurrection, you have a new nature.

> [11] *In the same way, count yourselves dead to sin but alive to God in Christ Jesus.* [12] *Therefore do not let sin reign in your mortal body so that you obey its evil desires.* [13] *Do not offer the parts of your body to sin, as instruments of wickedness, but rather offer yourselves to God, as those who have been brought from death to life; and offer the parts of your body to him as instruments of righteousness.* (Romans 6:11–13 NIV)

DISCOVERY QUESTIONS

1. Most of us are frustrated by the daily battle we face with sin. What is the difference between a life of faith in Christ and a life based on willpower? Discuss what each one looks like. How do you think facing your daily battles through faith in God, rather than with personal willpower alone, could make a difference in your daily life?

2. What would it take for you to see yourself as the new person Christ has made you to be? How can the group support you in your commitment?

3. When we belong to Christ, Satan loses the power to control us; we are no longer obliged to obey him. Who do you know that needs to hear this good news?

Did You Get It? How has this week's study helped you better understand the two natures each Christian must deal with?

Share with Someone: Think of a person you can encourage with the truth you learned in this session. Write their name in the space below and pray for God to provide that opportunity this week.

LIVING ON PURPOSE
Discipleship

This week's exercise for spiritual growth is **fasting**. The real purpose of fasting is not self-denial—because the Bible teaches us in Colossians 3 that self-denial doesn't bring about spiritual growth—but a change of activity that gives new motivation and more time to focus on God. There are two ways you can do this:

1. **Go on a one-day fast.** Fasting usually means giving up food. Drink juices and water, but don't eat anything for one day. Use the time that you would usually use to prepare and eat meals to focus on God.

Some people shouldn't give up food for a day—it isn't a healthy decision for anyone with blood sugar issues, for example. Consider this instead:

2. **Commit to an "entertainment" fast.** For one day, don't turn on the TV, the radio in the car, your MP3 player, or any other entertainment medium. Use the time you would have spent on entertainment to focus on God.

PRAYER DIRECTION

Thank God for each of the wonderful pictures of our new life in Christ that he has provided in his Word and for what they mean to you personally.

"HOW TO BECOME A FOLLOWER OF JESUS CHRIST"

Have you ever surrendered your life to Jesus Christ? Take a few minutes with your group to watch a brief video by Pastor Rick Warren on how to become part of the family of God. It is included on the Main Menu of this DVD.

3

Session three

THE POWER OF GRACE

CATCHING UP

1. Last week we learned that, in Christ, sin no longer has power over us. Did you get an opportunity to share this exciting truth with someone?

2. What did you learn during last week's "Living on Purpose" activity on fasting?

Key Verse

You began your life in Christ by the Spirit. Now are you trying to make it complete by your own power? That is foolish.

Galatians 3:3 (NCV)

BIBLE TEACHING
Watch the video lesson now and take notes in your outline on pages 21-23.

The Power of _____ over the _____

Just as we are justified by faith and grace, we are sanctified by faith and grace.

> *You began your life in Christ by the Spirit. Now are you trying to make it complete by your own power? That is foolish.*
> (Galatians 3:3 NCV)

> *As you received Christ Jesus the Lord, so continue to live in him. [We received Jesus into our lives by grace, and we live our lives in him by grace.]* (Colossians 2:6 NCV)

By faith you can say, "I am _____ from the law."

> *Through Christ Jesus the law of the Spirit that brings life made me free from the law that brings sin and death.*
> (Romans 8:2 NCV)

> *That old law had glory, but it really loses its glory when it is compared to the much greater glory of this new way.*
> (2 Corinthians 3:10 NCV)

By faith you can say, "I have a _____ ."

> *Now you are free from sin, your old master, and you have become slaves to your new master, righteousness.*
> (Romans 6:18 NLT)

The _____ of Growth

By faith you ask God to _____ .

> ^{22}You were taught, with regard to your former way of life, to
> put off your old self, which is being corrupted by its deceitful
> desires; ^{23}to be made new in the attitude of your minds;
> ^{24}and to put on the new self, created to be like God in true
> righteousness and holiness. (Ephesians 4:22–24 NIV)

Being renewed in your mind is the often forgotten step in the process
of putting off the old and putting on the new. Inner renewal is key to
outer transformation.

> Do not conform any longer to the pattern of this world, but be
> transformed by the renewing of your mind. Then you will be
> able to test and approve what God's will is—his good, pleasing
> and perfect will. (Romans 12:2 NIV)

> Therefore we do not lose heart. Though outwardly we are
> wasting away, yet inwardly we are being renewed day by day.
> (2 Corinthians 4:16 NIV)

Ephesians 4:25–32 helps us see that a key aspect of this inner renewal is
the ability to see God's positive reasons for making a change. A renewed
mind has the ability to see things the way that God sees them.

Put off the old self	Put on the new self	Renewed in your minds
Put off falsehood . . .	. . . speak truthfully to his neighbor . . .	. . . for we are all members of one body.
In your anger do not sin . . .	. . . do not let the sun go down while you are still angry . . .	. . . do not give the devil a foothold.
He who has been stealing must steal no longer . . .	. . . but must work . . .	. . . that he may have something to share with those in need.
Do not let any unwholesome talk come out of your mouths . . .	. . . but only what is helpful for building others up . . .	. . . do not grieve the Holy Spirit.
Get rid of all bitterness, rage and anger, brawling and slander . . .	. . . be kind and compassionate to one another, forgiving each other . . .	. . . just as in Christ God forgave you.

DISCOVERY QUESTIONS

1. What do you think is the greatest benefit of living under grace rather than under the law? What are some ways people abuse God's grace? Is there an area of your life where you have been guilty of abusing the grace of God or of failing to recognize it?

2. As Christians, we understand that Christ comes into our lives by grace. In spite of that knowledge, why do you think we often fail to live by grace and live instead by works?

3. How can your small group help you live according to grace and no longer resort to legalistically following the law or requiring others to do the same? Is there anything you need to share with the group or your spiritual partner so they can hold you accountable for growth in this area?

4. What are two or three practical things that you could do to cooperate more fully with God in his desire to renew your mind?

Did You Get It? How has this week's study helped you better understand God's daily process of growth in your life?

Share with Someone: Think of a person you can encourage with the truth you learned in this session. Write their name in the space below and pray for God to provide that opportunity this week.

LIVING ON PURPOSE
Discipleship

This week's focus is on **generosity**. For this exercise, take a $20 bill and fold it in your wallet or purse to be ready to give to someone outside your group this week. (The amount may be adjusted depending on the finances of your group, but make it the same for all the group members.) Watch this week for an opportunity to give that bill to someone. Ask God to prompt you, showing you where his grace is most needed by someone in your local area. You can give the money anonymously or let the person know you're giving it and why—whichever you feel would best meet that person's need.

PRAYER DIRECTION

Take some time as a group to talk about your specific prayer requests and to pray for one another. Thank God for each of the wonderful pictures of grace he has provided in his Word and what they mean to you personally.

Are there any answers to last week's prayers to report? If so, celebrate these responses from God.

Session four

4

THE DAILY PROCESS
OF GROWTH

CATCHING UP

1. Who did you share last week's truth with?

2. What did you learn during last week's "Living on Purpose" activity on generosity?

Key Verse

. . . discipline yourself for the purpose of godliness.

1 Timothy 4:7b (NASB)

> ### BIBLE TEACHING
> Watch the video lesson now and take notes in your outline on pages 29–31.

The Daily Process of Growth (continued)

By faith you practice the _____ .

> *Spend your time and energy in training yourself for spiritual fitness.* (1 Timothy 4:7b NLT)

A CLOSER LOOK
Spiritual Disciplines

Three of the most important disciplines God uses to sanctify us are:

1. A _____ quiet time—in God's Word and prayer

   Jesus answered, "It is written: 'Man does not live on bread alone, but on every word that comes from the mouth of God.'" (Matthew 4:4 NIV)

2. A _____ tithe to God

   "Bring the whole tithe into the storehouse, that there may be food in my house. Test me in this," says the LORD Almighty, "and see if I will not throw open the floodgates of heaven and pour out so much blessing that you will not have room enough for it." (Malachi 3:10 NIV)

3. A _____ commitment to a small group

   So now you Gentiles are no longer strangers and foreigners. You are citizens along with all of God's holy people. You are members of God's family. (Ephesians 2:19 NLT)

By faith you choose to trust God in the _____

_____ .

God has allowed our choice to be one of the key factors in our growth. One of the most important choices we make is our response to the difficulties and trials we all face as a part of life.

> *²Dear brothers, is your life full of difficulties and temptations? Then be happy, ³for when the way is rough, your patience has a chance to grow. ⁴So let it grow, and don't try to squirm out of your problems. For when your patience is finally in full bloom, then you will be ready for anything, strong in character, full and complete.* (James 1:2–4 LB)

God's Promise to _____

> *²⁸We know that in everything God works for the good of those who love him. They are the people he called, because that was his plan. ²⁹God knew them before he made the world, and he decided that they would be like his Son so that Jesus would be the firstborn of many brothers.* (Romans 8:28–29 NCV)

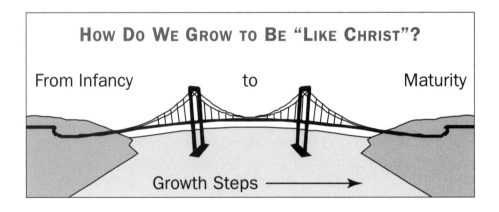

HOW DO WE GROW TO BE "LIKE CHRIST"?

From Infancy   to   Maturity

Growth Steps ⟶

THE DAILY PROCESS OF GROWTH

By faith you believe in _____ to accomplish his work in your life.

You are not alone. God is working for your growth. He is working to make you like his Son, Jesus.

- God is _____ to your growth.

    "and I consecrate myself to meet their need for growth in truth and holiness." (John 17:19 LB)

    Long ago, even before he made the world, God chose us to be his very own, through what Christ would do for us; he decided then to make us holy in his eyes, without a single fault—we who stand before him covered with his love. (Ephesians 1:4 LB)

- God _____ us and is _____ for us to be sanctified.

    . . . he who began a good work in you will carry it on to completion until the day of Christ Jesus. (Philippians 1:6 NIV)

KEY PERSONAL PERSPECTIVE
A Matter of Trust

Growth is not accomplished by _____ , but by _____ .

Trust means we work out what God works in.

[12] . . . continue to work out your salvation with fear and trembling, [13]for it is God who works in you to will and to act according to his good purpose. (Philippians 2:12–13 NIV)

[24,25]And now—all glory to him who alone is God, who saves me through Jesus Christ our Lord; yes, splendor and majesty, all power and authority are his from the beginning; his they are and his they evermore shall be. And he is able to keep you from slipping and falling away, and to bring you, sinless and perfect, into his glorious presence with mighty shouts of everlasting joy . . . (Jude 24–25 LB)

DISCOVERY QUESTIONS

1. The three important disciplines of spiritual growth shared in this session are: 1) daily quiet time, 2) weekly tithe, and 3) regular commitment to a small group. Share how these habits have helped you to grow spiritually. How are you personally practicing each habit?

2. Which of these disciplines for spiritual growth do you have the most difficulty making a regular habit?

3. God also uses the circumstances of our lives for our growth. What is the greatest lesson you have learned in difficult times?

4. The goal of becoming completely like Christ will never be fully realized by any of us while on this earth. What are some practical and personal ways you use to keep from getting discouraged as you reach for a goal you know you won't achieve until you get to heaven?

Did You Get It? How has this week's study helped you see you can trust God to grow you throughout all the days of your life?

Share with Someone: Think of a person you can encourage with the truth you learned in this session. Write their name in the space below and pray for God to provide that opportunity this week.

LIVING ON PURPOSE
Discipleship

This week's spiritual growth exercise is on **confession**. Use the "Cleansing for Personal Renewal" list on pages 35–37 to think through possible sins in your life.

1. As you are reminded of a specific sin or area of sin, write it down on a blank sheet of paper. You may end up with just a few or you may fill the page! Whatever the length of your list, the wonderful truth is that through our repentance and trust in the forgiveness of Christ every sin is forgiven!

2. Claim the truth of 1 John 1:9 (NLT): *But if we confess our sins to him, he is faithful and just to forgive us and to cleanse us from every wrong.*

3. Next, destroy the list, in recognition of the truth that Jesus has forgiven and cleansed you.

If any of the sins required relational or financial restitution, determine to make amends, give apologies, or pay back what was taken.

PRAYER DIRECTION

As a group, pray Jude 24–25 for each other in faith and gratitude for the work that God is doing in your lives. Go around the room, and pray for the person on your right, inserting his or her name in the blanks:

And now—all glory to you alone, God, who saved _____ *through Jesus Christ our Lord. Thank you that you are able to keep* _____ *from slipping and falling away, and to bring* _____ *, sinless and perfect, into your glorious presence with mighty shouts of everlasting joy!*

CLEANSING FOR PERSONAL RENEWAL

The following is a list of common sins that prevent God from blessing and using our lives. As you prayerfully read this list, examine yourself and circle or underline the areas that apply to you.

23Search me, O God, and know my heart; test my thoughts.
24Point out anything you find in me that makes you sad, and
lead me along the path of everlasting life. (Psalm 139:23–24 LB)

But how can I ever know what sins are lurking in my heart?
Cleanse me from these hidden faults. (Psalm 19:12 LB)

Take time to read each passage and ask God to show you your reflection in his mirror.

Matthew 6:12–14 — Your Relationships to Others

Have you been holding a grudge against anyone? Have you been secretly unforgiving? Desiring revenge? Secretly jealous of someone? Harboring bitterness? Unwilling to forget a misunderstanding? Hateful? Do you avoid people whom you dislike but need your love? Are you critical or judging of others? Do you justify your bad attitude by claiming it is someone else's fault? Do you gossip to feel superior or better about yourself? Have you worn a self-protective mask and failed to let people get close to you?

Matthew 6:33 — Your Priorities

In what areas of your life have you failed to put God first? Do any of the following interfere with doing God's will—your personal ambitions and goals, your fun and hobbies, your job, your desire to get rich, your own plans, your habits, your friendships, your family? Do you find you don't have time for God? For prayer? For Bible reading? For small group? Have other activities made you regularly miss worship with other believers? Is there anything you would be unwilling to give up if God asked?

Ephesians 4:31 — Attitudes

Do you complain about your circumstances? Are you ungrateful? Irritable or cranky? Always speak negatively? Do you get angry easily and blow up or pout? Are you ever harsh or unkind? Unteachable? Sarcastic? Do you put down others instead of building them up? Do you worry about things God wants you to trust him with? Are you fearful or anxious? Do you try to control people or circumstances? Are you impatient? Prideful or stubborn?

Colossians 3:9 — Integrity

Are you honest in all your dealings? Do you find it easy to lie? Do you exaggerate to make yourself look better? Leave a better impression of yourself than is true? Have you cheated on taxes? Have you stolen things? Failed to return things? Do you do good things hoping to impress others? Do you pretend to live one way in front of your Christian friends and another way at home or at work? Do you keep your promises? Are you dependable?

Romans 12:1–2 — Your Mind

Have you failed to guard your mind from unhealthy, ungodly input? Have you filled your mind with sleazy or profane movies, television programs, magazines, or books? Do you participate in entertainment that causes you to have impure thoughts? Pornography? Do you spend more time with the TV or the Internet than with God's Word? Are you lazy in memorizing Scripture verses?

Acts 20:35 — Your Money and Possessions

Have you failed to dedicate all of your possessions to the Lord? Have you acted like your possessions belong to you, not God? Have you robbed God by not giving him the 10 percent tithe that he commands? Do you find yourself resentful or defensive when asked to give to God's work? Are you eager to get rich? Are you stingy with wealth? Have you failed to trust God with your finances? Do you need to be more generous with what God has given you?

1 Corinthians 6:19–20 — Your Body

Are you in any way careless with your body or health? Is there any activity or habit that is harmful to you? Are you lazy or undisciplined?

2 Corinthians 5:7 — Walking by Faith

Do you tend to follow your moods or feelings rather than doing what you know is right? Do you allow your emotions to be inspired for the Lord at church but then do nothing about it? Do you focus more on your circumstances instead of the promises of God? Have you failed to trust God with the disappointments of your life?

Hebrews 10:25 — Your Church Family and Ministry

Are you accountable to any small group of believers for growth? Are you using your God-given S.H.A.P.E. — your Spiritual gifts, Heart, Abilities, Personality, and Experiences — in some ministry? Do you pray for your church and your pastors? Have you been critical instead of helpful? Have you expected to be "fed" without giving back?

Joshua 24:15 — Your Family

Are you unkind to those you live with? Do you pray for them? Do you need to ask forgiveness from a family member? Have you been unfaithful to your spouse mentally, emotionally, or physically?

Acts 20:24 — Your Mission In The World

Have you failed to share the good news of Christ with your relatives? With friends? With coworkers? With neighbors? Have you kept silent in fear?

Ask God to remind you of anything that has hindered his blessing on your life. "But if we confess our sins to him, he can be depended on to forgive us and to cleanse us from every wrong" (1 John 1:9a LB).

NOTES

Small Group Resources

HELPS FOR HOSTS

Top Ten Ideas for New Hosts

Congratulations! As the host of your small group, you have responded to the call to help shepherd Jesus' flock. Few other tasks in the family of God surpass the contribution you will be making.

As you prepare to facilitate your group, whether it is one session or the entire series, here are a few thoughts to keep in mind. We encourage you to read and review these tips with each new discussion host before he or she leads.

Remember you are not alone. God knows everything about you, and he knew you would be asked to facilitate your group. Even though you may not feel ready, this is common for all good hosts. God promises, *"I will never leave you; I will never abandon you"* (Hebrews 13:5 TEV). Whether you are facilitating for one evening, several weeks, or a lifetime, you will be blessed as you serve.

1. **Don't try to do it alone.** Pray right now for God to help you build a healthy team. If you can enlist a cohost to help you shepherd the group, you will find your experience much richer. This is your chance to involve as many people as you can in building a healthy group. All you have to do is ask people to help. You'll be surprised at the response.

2. **Be friendly and be yourself.** God wants to use your unique gifts and temperament. Be sure to greet people at the door with a big smile . . . this can set the mood for the whole gathering. Remember, they are taking as big a step to show up at your house as you are to lead this group! Don't try to do things exactly like another host; do them in a way that fits you. Admit when you don't have an answer and apologize when you make a mistake. Your group will love you for it and you'll sleep better at night.

3. **Prepare for your meeting ahead of time.** Review the session and write down your responses to each question. Pay special attention to exercises that ask group members to do something other than engage in discussion. These exercises will help your group live what the Bible teaches, not just talk about it. Be sure you understand how an exercise works. If the exercise employs one of the items in the Small Group Resources section (such as the Group Guidelines), be sure to look over that item so you'll know how it works.

4. **Pray for your group members by name.** Before you begin your session, take a few moments and pray for each member by name. You may want to review the prayer list at least once a week. Ask God to use your time together to touch the heart of every person in your group. Expect God to lead you to whomever he wants you to encourage or challenge in a special way. If you listen, God will surely lead.

5. **When you ask a question, be patient.** Someone will eventually respond. Sometimes people need a moment or two of silence to think about the question. If silence doesn't bother you, it won't bother anyone else. After someone responds, affirm the response with a simple "thanks" or "great answer." Then ask, "How about somebody else?" or "Would someone who hasn't shared like to add anything?" Be sensitive to new people or reluctant members who aren't ready to say, pray, or do anything. If you give them a safe setting, they will blossom over time. If someone in your group is a "wallflower" who sits silently through every session, consider talking to them privately and encouraging them to participate. Let them know how important they are to you—that they are loved and appreciated—and that the group would value their input. Remember, still water often runs deep.

6. **Provide transitions between questions.** Ask if anyone would like to read the paragraph or Bible passage. Don't call on anyone, but ask for a volunteer, and then be patient until someone begins. Be sure to thank the person who reads aloud.

7. **Break into smaller groups occasionally.** With a greater opportunity to talk in a small circle, people will connect more with the study, apply more quickly what they're learning, and ultimately get more out of their small group experience. A small circle also encourages a quiet person to participate and tends to minimize the effects of a more vocal or dominant member.

8. **Small circles are also helpful during prayer time.** People who are unaccustomed to praying aloud will feel more comfortable trying it with just two or three others. Also, prayer requests won't take as much time, so circles will have more time to actually pray. When you gather back with the whole group, you can have one person from each circle briefly update everyone on the prayer requests from their subgroups. The other great aspect of subgrouping is that it fosters leadership development. As you ask people in the group to facilitate discussion or to lead a prayer circle, it gives them a small leadership step that can build their confidence.

9. **Rotate facilitators occasionally.** You may be perfectly capable of hosting each time, but you will help others grow in their faith and gifts if you give them opportunities to host the group.

10. **One final challenge (for new or first-time hosts).** Before your first opportunity to lead, look up each of the six passages that follow. Read each one as a devotional exercise to help prepare you with a shepherd's heart. Trust us on this one. If you do this, you will be more than ready for your first meeting.

Matthew 9:36–38 (NIV)
36When Jesus saw the crowds, he had compassion on them, because they were harassed and helpless, like sheep without a shepherd. 37Then he said to his disciples, "The harvest is plentiful but the workers are few. 38Ask the Lord of the harvest, therefore, to send out workers into his harvest field."

John 10:14–15 (NIV)
14I am the good shepherd; I know my sheep and my sheep know me—15just as the Father knows me and I know the Father—and I lay down my life for the sheep.

1 Peter 5:2–4 (NIV)

[2]*Be shepherds of God's flock that is under your care, serving as overseers—not because you must, but because you are willing, as God wants you to be;* [3]*not greedy for money, but eager to serve; not lording it over those entrusted to you, but being examples to the flock.* [4]*And when the Chief Shepherd appears, you will receive the crown of glory that will never fade away.*

Philippians 2:1–5 (NIV)

[1]*If you have any encouragement from being united with Christ, if any comfort from his love, if any fellowship with the Spirit, if any tenderness and compassion,* [2]*then make my joy complete by being like-minded, having the same love, being one in spirit and purpose.* [3]*Do nothing out of selfish ambition or vain conceit, but in humility consider others better than yourselves.* [4]*Each of you should look not only to your own interests, but also to the interests of others.* [5]*Your attitude should be the same as that of Jesus Christ.*

Hebrews 10:23–25 (NIV)

[23]*Let us hold unswervingly to the hope we profess, for he who promised is faithful.* [24]*And let us consider how we may spur one another on toward love and good deeds.* [25]*Let us not give up meeting together, as some are in the habit of doing, but let us encourage one another—and all the more as you see the Day approaching.*

1 Thessalonians 2:7–8, 11–12 (NIV)

[7]*. . . but we were gentle among you, like a mother caring for her little children.* [8]*We loved you so much that we were delighted to share with you not only the gospel of God but our lives as well, because you had become so dear to us. . . .* [11]*For you know that we dealt with each of you as a father deals with his own children,* [12]*encouraging, comforting and urging you to live lives worthy of God, who calls you into his kingdom and glory.*

FREQUENTLY ASKED QUESTIONS

How long will this group meet?

This volume of *Foundations: Sanctification* is four sessions long. We encourage your group to add a fifth session for a celebration. In your final session, each group member may decide if he or she desires to continue on for another study. At that time you may also want to do some informal evaluation, discuss your Group Guidelines, and decide which study you want to do next. We recommend you visit our website at **www.saddlebackresources.com** for more video-based small group studies.

Who is the host?

The host is the person who coordinates and facilitates your group meetings. In addition to a host, we encourage you to select one or more group members to lead your group discussions. Several other responsibilities can be rotated, including refreshments, prayer requests, worship, or keeping up with those who miss a meeting. Shared ownership in the group helps everybody grow.

Where do we find new group members?

Recruiting new members can be a challenge for groups, especially new groups with just a few people, or existing groups that lose a few people along the way. We encourage you to use the *Circles of Life* diagram on page 48 of this DVD study guide to brainstorm a list of people from your workplace, church, school, neighborhood, family, and so on. Then pray for the people on each member's list. Allow each member to invite several people from their list. Some groups fear that newcomers will interrupt the intimacy that members have built over time. However, groups that welcome newcomers generally gain strength with the infusion of new blood. Remember, the next person you add just might become a friend for eternity. Logistically, groups find different ways to add members. Some groups remain permanently open, while others choose to open periodically, such as at the beginning or end of a study. If your group becomes too large for easy, face-to-face conversations, you can subgroup, forming a second discussion group in another room.

How do we handle the child care needs in our group?

Child care needs must be handled very carefully. This is a sensitive issue. We suggest you seek creative solutions as a group. One common solution is to have the adults meet in the living room and share the cost of a babysitter (or two) who can be with the kids in another part of the house. Another popular option is to have one home for the kids and a second home (close by) for the adults. If desired, the adults could rotate the responsibility of providing a lesson for the kids. This last option is great with school-age kids and can be a huge blessing to families.

GROUP GUIDELINES

It's a good idea for every group to put words to their shared values, expectations, and commitments. Such guidelines will help you avoid unspoken agendas and unmet expectations. We recommend you discuss your guidelines during Session One in order to lay the foundation for a healthy group experience. Feel free to modify anything that does not work for your group.

We agree to the following values:

Clear Purpose To grow healthy spiritual lives by building a healthy small group community

Group Attendance To give priority to the group meeting (call if I am absent or late)

Safe Environment To create a safe place where people can be heard and feel loved (no quick answers, snap judgments, or simple fixes)

Be Confidential To keep anything that is shared strictly confidential and within the group

Conflict Resolution To avoid gossip and to immediately resolve any concerns by following the principles of Matthew 18:15–17

Spiritual Health To give group members permission to speak into my life and help me live a healthy, balanced spiritual life that is pleasing to God

Limit Our Freedom To limit our freedom by not serving or consuming alcohol during small group meetings or events so as to avoid causing a weaker brother or sister to stumble (1 Corinthians 8:1–13; Romans 14:19–21)

Welcome Newcomers   To invite friends who might benefit from this study and warmly welcome newcomers

Building Relationships To get to know the other members of the group and pray for them regularly

Other   _____

We have also discussed and agreed on the following items:

Child Care

_____

_____

Starting Time

_____

Ending Time

_____

If you haven't already done so, take a few minutes to fill out the *Small Group Calendar* on page 52.

CIRCLES OF LIFE—SMALL GROUP CONNECTIONS

Discover who you can connect in community

Use this chart to help carry out one of the values in the Group Guidelines, to "Welcome Newcomers."

"Follow me, and I will make you fishers of men." (Matthew 4:19 KJV)

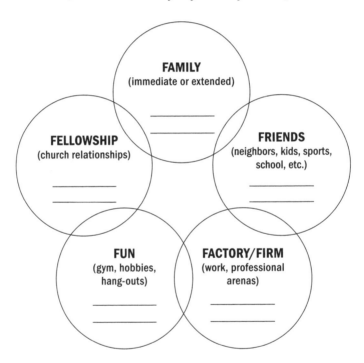

Follow this simple three-step process:

1. List 1–2 people in each circle.

2. Prayerfully select one person or couple from your list and tell your group about them.

3. Give them a call and invite them to your next meeting. Over 50 percent of those invited to a small group say, "Yes!"

SMALL GROUP PRAYER AND PRAISE REPORT

This is a place where you can write each other's requests for prayer. You can also make a note when God answers a prayer. Pray for each other's requests. If you're new to group prayer, it's okay to pray silently or to pray by using just one sentence: "God, please help

_____ to _____."

DATE	PERSON	PRAYER REQUEST	PRAISE REPORT

SMALL GROUP PRAYER AND PRAISE REPORT

DATE	PERSON	PRAYER REQUEST	PRAISE REPORT

SMALL GROUP PRAYER AND PRAISE REPORT

DATE	PERSON	PRAYER REQUEST	PRAISE REPORT

SMALL GROUP CALENDAR

Healthy groups share responsibilities and group ownership. It might take some time for this to develop. Shared ownership ensures that responsibility for the group doesn't fall to one person. Use the calendar to keep track of social events, mission projects, birthdays, or days off. Complete this calendar at your first or second meeting. Planning ahead will increase attendance and shared ownership.

DATE	LESSON	LOCATION	FACILITATOR	SNACK OR MEAL
5/4	Session 2	Chris and Andrea	Jim Brown	Phil and Karen

Answer Key

Session One:
Two Focuses of Sanctification

1. <u>Justified</u>—Declared eternally not guilty.
2. <u>Sanctified</u>—Being set apart for holiness.
3. <u>Glorified</u>—The completed act of our being with God for eternity.

Sanctified means <u>set apart</u>.

I am a <u>growing</u> saint.

The <u>finished action</u> of being made holy

The <u>daily process</u> of becoming holy

1. Sanctification is <u>once</u> and <u>complete</u>.
2. Sanctification is <u>continual</u> and <u>progressive</u>.

Session Two:
The Two Natures of the Christian

You have both an <u>old</u> nature and a <u>new</u> nature.

1. You express faith concerning your new nature when you see yourself as <u>a new person</u>.

   - I was "<u>in Adam</u>."
   - I am now "<u>in Christ</u>."

   1. You don't have to <u>achieve</u> your new life.
   2. You don't have to work to <u>keep</u> your new life.

2. You express faith concerning your old nature when you see yourself as <u>dead to sin</u>.

   - Not by <u>ignoring</u> it
   - Not by <u>human effort</u>
   - By faith in what <u>God has done</u>

3. You express faith concerning both your new and old natures when you see yourself with a <u>new power</u> to overcome evil.

   - Before salvation, I belonged to <u>Satan</u>.
   - After salvation, I belong to <u>God</u>.
   - Because I belong to God, Satan has no power to <u>control me</u>.

Session Three:
The Power of Grace

The Power of <u>Grace</u> over the <u>Law</u>

By faith you can say, "I am <u>free</u> from the law."

By faith you can say, "I have a <u>new master</u>."

The <u>Daily Process</u> of Growth

By faith you ask God to <u>renew your mind</u>.

Session Four:
The Daily Process of Growth

By faith you practice the <u>disciplines of growth</u>.

1. A <u>daily</u> quiet time—in God's Word and prayer
2. A <u>weekly</u> tithe to God
3. A <u>regular</u> commitment to a small group

By faith you choose to trust God in the <u>circumstances of life</u>.

God's Promise to <u>Finish His Work</u>

By faith you believe in <u>God's ability</u> to accomplish his work in your life.

   - God is <u>committed</u> to your growth.
   - God <u>wants</u> us and is <u>working</u> for us to be sanctified.

Growth is not accomplished by <u>trying hard</u>, but by <u>trusting him</u>.

NOTES

KEY VERSES

One of the most effective ways to drive deeply into our lives the principles we are learning in this series is to memorize key Scriptures. For many, memorization is a new concept or one that has been difficult in the past. We encourage you to stretch yourself and try to memorize these four key verses. If possible, memorize these as a group and make them part of your group time. You may cut these apart and carry them in your wallet.

I have hidden your word in my heart that I might not sin against you.

Psalm 119:11 (NIV)

Session One

With one sacrifice he made perfect forever those who are being made holy.

Hebrews 10:14 (NCV)

Session Two

I have been crucified with Christ and I no longer live, but Christ lives in me. The life I live in the body, I live by faith in the Son of God, who loved me and gave himself for me.

Galatians 2:20 (NIV)

Session Three

You began your life in Christ by the Spirit. Now are you trying to make it complete by your own power? That is foolish.

Galatians 3:3 (NCV)

Session Four

. . . discipline yourself for the purpose of godliness.

1 Timothy 4:7b (NASB)

NOTES

We value your thoughts about what you've just read.
Please share them with us. You'll find contact information
in the back of this book.

The Purpose Driven® Life
A six-session video-based study for groups or individuals

Embark on a journey of discovery with this video-based study taught by Rick Warren. In it you will discover the answer to life's most fundamental question: "What on earth am I here for?"

And here's a clue to the answer: It's not about you . . . You were created by God and for God, and until you understand that, life will never make sense. It is only in God that we discover our origin, our identity, our meaning, our purpose, our significance, and our destiny."

Whether you experience this adventure with a small group or on your own, this six-session, video-based study will change your life.

DVD Study Guide: 978-0-310-27866-5
DVD: 978-0-310-27864-1

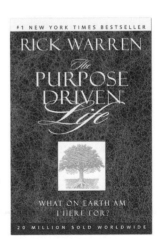

Be sure to combine this study with your reading of the best-selling book, *The Purpose Driven® Life,* to give you or your small group the opportunity to discuss the implications and applications of living the life God created you to live.

Hardcover, Jacketed: 978-0-310-20571-5
Softcover: 978-0-310-27699-9

Pick up a copy today at your favorite bookstore!

ZONDERVAN®
.com

Foundations: 11 Core Truths to Build Your Life On

Taught by Tom Holladay and Kay Warren

Foundations is a series of 11 four-week video studies covering the most important, foundational doctrines of the Christian faith. Study topics include:

The Bible—This study focuses on where the Bible came from, why it can be trusted, and how it can change your life.
DVD Study Guide: 978-0-310-27670-8
DVD: 978-0-310-27669-2

God—This study focuses not just on facts about God, but on how to know God himself in a more powerful and personal way.
DVD Study Guide: 978-0-310-27672-2
DVD: 978-0-310-27671-5

Jesus—As we look at what the Bible says about the person of Christ, we do so as people who are developing a lifelong relationship with Jesus.
DVD Study Guide: 978-0-310-27674-6
DVD: 978-0-310-27673-9

The Holy Spirit—This study focuses on the person, the presence, and the power of the Holy Spirit, and how you can be filled with the Holy Spirit on a daily basis.
DVD Study Guide: 978-0-310-27676-0
DVD: 978-0-310-27675-3

Creation—Each of us was personally created by a loving God. This study does not shy away from the great scientific and theological arguments that surround the creation/evolution debate. However, you will find the goal of this study is deepening your awareness of God as your Creator.
DVD Study Guide: 978-0-310-27678-4
DVD: 978-0-310-27677-7

Pick up a copy today at your favorite bookstore!

ZONDERVAN®
.com

Salvation—This study focuses on God's solution to man's need for salvation, what Jesus Christ did for us on the cross, and the assurance and security of God's love and provision for eternity.

DVD Study Guide: 978-0-310-27682-1
DVD: 978-0-310-27679-1

Sanctification—This study focuses on the two natures of the Christian. We'll see the difference between grace and law, and how these two things work in our lives.

DVD Study Guide: 978-0-310-27684-5
DVD: 978-0-310-27683-8

Good and Evil—Why do bad things happen to good people? Through this study we'll see how and why God continues to allow evil to exist. The ultimate goal is to build up our faith and relationship with God as we wrestle with these difficult questions.

DVD Study Guide: 978-0-310-27687-6
DVD: 978-0-310-27686-9

The Afterlife—The Bible does not answer all the questions we have about what happens to us after we die; however, this study deals with what the Bible does tell us. This important study gives us hope and helps us move from a focus on the here and now to a focus on eternity.

DVD Study Guide: 978-0-310-27689-0
DVD: 978-0-310-27688-3

The Church—This study focuses on the birth of the church, the nature of the church, and the mission of the church.

DVD Study Guide: 978-0-310-27692-0
DVD: 978-0-310-27691-3

The Second Coming—This study addresses both the hope and the uncertainties surrounding the second coming of Jesus Christ.

DVD Study Guide: 978-0-310-27695-1
DVD: 978-0-310-27693-7

Pick up a copy today at your favorite bookstore!

Celebrate Recovery, Updated Curriculum Kit

This kit will provide your church with the tools necessary to start a successful Celebrate Recovery program. *Kit includes:*

- Introductory Guide for Leaders DVD
- Leader's Guide
- 4 Participant's Guides (one of each guide)
- CD-ROM with 25 lessons
- CD-ROM with sermon transcripts
- 4-volume audio CD sermon series

Curriculum Kit: 978-0-310-26847-5

Participant's Guide 4-pack

The Celebrate Recovery Participant's Guide 4-pack is a convenient resource when you're just getting started or if you need replacement guides for your program.

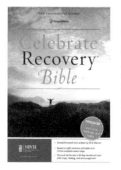

Celebrate Recovery Bible

With features based on eight principles Jesus voiced in his Sermon on the Mount, the new *Celebrate Recovery Bible* offers hope, encouragement, and empowerment for those struggling with the circumstances of their lives and the habits they are trying to control.

Hardcover 978-0-310-92849-2
Softcover 978-0-310-93810-1

Stepping Out of Denial into God's Grace

Participant's Guide 1 introduces the eight principles of recovery based on Jesus' words in the Beatitudes, and focuses on principles 1–3. Participants learn about denial, hope, sanity, and more.

Getting Right with God, Yourself, and Others

Participant's Guide 3 covers principles 5–7 based on Jesus' words in the Beatitudes. With courage and support from their fellow participants, people seeking recovery will find victory, forgiveness, and grace.

Taking an Honest and Spiritual Inventory

Participant's Guide 2 focuses on the fourth principle based on Jesus' words in the Beatitudes and builds on the Scripture, *"Happy are the pure in heart."* (Matthew 5:8) The participant will learn an invaluable principle for recovery and also take an in-depth spiritual inventory.

Growing in Christ While Helping Others

Participant's Guide 4 walks through the final steps of the eight recovery principles based on Jesus' words in the Beatitudes. In this final phase, participants learn to move forward in newfound freedom in Christ, learning how to give back to others. There's even a practical lesson called "Seven reasons we get stuck in our recoveries."

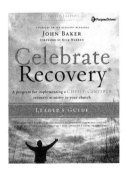

Leader's Guide

The Celebrate Recovery Leader's Guide gives you everything you need to facilitate your preparation time. Virtually walking you through every meeting, the Leader's Guide is a must-have for every leader on your Celebrate Recovery ministry team.

Pick up a copy today at your favorite bookstore!

ZONDERVAN®
.com

Wide Angle: Framing Your Worldview

Christianity is much more than a religion. It is a worldview—a way of seeing all of life and the world around you. Your worldview impacts virtually every decision you make in life: moral decisions, relational decisions, financial decisions— everything. How you see the world determines how you face the world.

In this brand new study, Rick Warren and Chuck Colson discuss such key issues as moral relativism, tolerance, terrorism, creationism vs. Darwinism, sin and suffering. They explore in depth the Christian worldview as it relates to the most important questions in life:

- Why does it matter what I believe?
- How do I know what's true?
- Where do I come from?
- Why is the world so messed up?
- Is there a solution?
- What is my purpose in life?

This study is as deep as it is wide, addressing vitally important topics for every follower of Christ.

Rick Warren

Chuck Colson

DVD Study Guide: 978-1-4228-0083-6
DVD: 978-1-4228-0082-9

The Way of a Worshiper

The pursuit of God is the chase of a lifetime—in fact, it's been going on since the day you were born. The question is: Have you been the hunter or the prey?

This small group study is not about music. It's not even about going to church. It's about living your life as an offering of worship to God. It's about tapping into the source of power to live the Christian life. And it's about discovering the secret to friendship with God.

In these four video sessions, Buddy Owens helps you unpack the meaning of worship. Through his very practical, engaging, and at times surprising insights, Buddy shares truths from Scripture and from life that will help you understand in a new and deeper way just what it means to be a worshiper.

God is looking for worshipers. His invitation to friendship is open and genuine. Will you take him up on his offer? Will you give yourself to him in worship? Then come walk *The Way of a Worshiper* and discover the secret to friendship with God.

DVD Study Guide: 978-1-4228-0096-6
DVD: 978-1-4228-0095-9

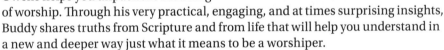

THE WAY of a WORSHIPER

Your study of this material will be greatly enhanced by reading the book, *The Way of a Worshiper: Discover the Secret to Friendship with God.*

Managing Our Finances God's Way

Did you know that there are over 2,350 verses in the Bible about money? Did you know that nearly half of Jesus' parables are about possessions? The Bible is packed with wise counsel about your financial life. In fact, Jesus had more to say about money than about heaven and hell combined.

Introducing a new video-based small group study that will inspire you to live debt free! Created by Saddleback Church and Crown Financial Ministries, learn what the Bible has to say about our finances from Rick Warren, Chip Ingram, Ron Blue, Howard Dayton, and Chuck Bentley as they address important topics like:

- God's Solution to Debt
- Saving and Investing
- Plan Your Spending
- Giving as an Act of Worship
- Enjoy What God Has Given You

Study includes:

- DVD with seven 20-minute lessons

- Workbook with seven lessons

- Resource CD with digital version of all worksheets that perform calculations automatically

- Contact information for help with answering questions

- Resources for keeping financial plans on track and making them lifelong habits

NOTE: PARTICIPANTS DO NOT SHARE PERSONAL FINANCIAL INFORMATION WITH EACH OTHER.

DVD Study Guide: 978-1-4228-0083-6
DVD: 978-1-4228-0082-9

Share Your Thoughts

With the Author: Your comments will be forwarded to
the author when you send them to *zauthor@zondervan.com*.

With Zondervan: Submit your review of this book
by writing to *zreview@zondervan.com*.

Free Online Resources at
www.zondervan.com/hello

 Zondervan AuthorTracker: Be notified whenever your
favorite authors publish new books, go on tour, or post
an update about what's happening in their lives.

 Daily Bible Verses and Devotions: Enrich your life
with daily Bible verses or devotions that help you start
every morning focused on God.

 Free Email Publications: Sign up for newsletters on
fiction, Christian living, church ministry, parenting, and
more.

 Zondervan Bible Search: Find and compare
Bible passages in a variety of translations at
www.zondervanbiblesearch.com.

 Other Benefits: Register yourself to receive online
benefits like coupons and special offers, or to participate
in research.